R is for Race

A Stock Car Alphabet

Written by Brad Herzog and Illustrated by Jane Gilltrap Bready

Sleeping Bear Press™

310 North Main Street, Suite 300
Chelsea, MI 48118
www.sleepingbearpress.com

THOMSON
★ ™
GALE

© 2006 Thomson Gale, a part of the Thomson Corporation.

Thomson, Star Logo and Sleeping Bear Press are trademarks
and Gale is a registered trademark used herein under license.

Printed and bound in China.

10 9 8 7 6 5 4 3 2 1

Library of Congress Cataloging-in-Publication Data

Herzog, Brad.
R is for race : a stock car alphabet / written by Brad Herzog ;
illustrated by Jane Gilltrap Bready.
p. cm.
Summary: "This book provides readers with details on the famous drivers,
history, and statistics from the sport of stock car racing. From A to Z topics
such as Bill France, Daytona, helmets, pit stops, and more are explained and
illustrated for readers of all ages"—Provided by publisher.
ISBN 1-58536-272-7
1. Stock car racing—Juvenile literature. 2. Alphabet books.
I. Bready, Jane Gilltrap. II. Title.

GV1029.9.S74H47 2006
796.72—dc22   2006000028

Almost ever since there have been automobiles, people have raced them. The first auto race in America took place in Illinois on Thanksgiving Day in 1895 when six cars raced just over 54 miles through the snow from the city of Chicago to the city of Evanston and back. Only two cars completed the race, and the winner finished in nearly eight hours! Fourteen years later, in 1909, America's original speedway hosted its first racing event. At the new Indianapolis Motor Speedway, driver Barney Oldfield set a world record by reaching a speed of 83.2 miles per hour. A few decades later, groups of men in the southeastern United States would occasionally race each other in souped-up versions of cars that were available to the general public. This was the beginning of stock car racing.

Another **A** is Bobby Allison. In 1988, he won stock car racing's biggest event, the Daytona 500, for the third time. His son, Davey, finished in second place.

A a

A is early Auto races
      held so long ago.
What was so speedy then
      now seems rather slow.

In the 1930s and 1940s, stock car races were often unorganized events run by dishonest race promoters on shoddy tracks. But driver Bill France had a vision of forming an organization that offered a set race schedule, safe racetracks, and professionally run events. On December 12, 1947, he met with other race promoters and formed NASCAR, which stands for the National Association for Stock Car Auto Racing.

The first NASCAR race, in February 1948, was a 150-mile event on a track that was half on a local road and half on a beach just south of Daytona Beach, Florida. There were 14,000 spectators. Today, with Bill Sr.'s grandson Brian in charge of NASCAR, stock car racing is the fastest-growing sport in the nation. More than 6 million spectators and nearly 200 million television viewers watched the 36 official races in NASCAR's top league, the Nextel Cup Series (formerly known as the Winston Cup Series).

"Big Bill" France, a banker's son,
found stock car racing's key.
He formed a league called NASCAR
and showed what the sport could B.

Three brands of cars competed in the Nextel Cup Series in 2005—the Chevrolet Monte Carlo, Dodge Charger, and Ford Taurus. Unlike your typical family car, these vehicles have no doors (drivers enter through a window opening), no side-view mirrors, no passenger seats, no horn, not even an ignition where you insert a key (drivers just flip a switch). Stock cars are built for speed, not endurance. They only last an average of three years.

C is also the Chase for the Championship. After every Nextel Cup event, points are given to drivers according to where they finished in the race. Heading into the last ten races of the year, the top ten drivers in the standings (and those within 400 points of the leader) have their point totals adjusted so that only five points separate each driver from the one behind him. This playoff-style format means that any of the top drivers could win the Nextel Cup Series championship.

C Multicolored speed machines—
   is for the Cars.
The drivers get fortune and fame,
but their rides are the real stars.

D is—what else?—Daytona,
where NASCAR got its start.
Its famous superspeedway
is a racing work of art.

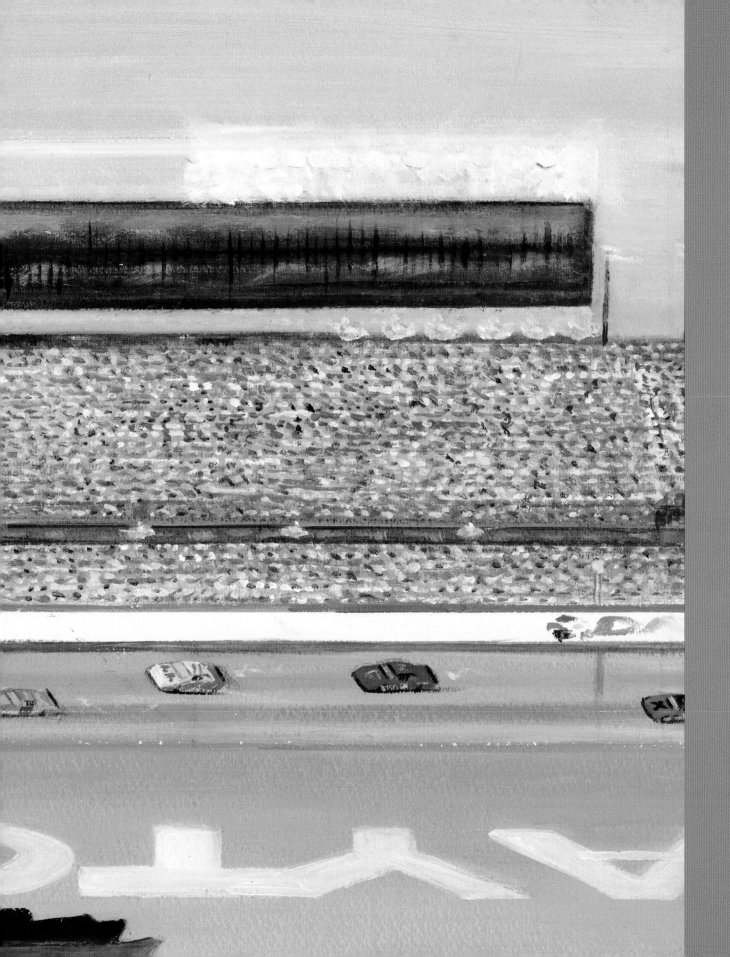

Daytona International Speedway is shaped like the letter **D**. It is located a few miles inland from where NASCAR's first race took place in Florida. Every February it hosts the Daytona 500, which is considered stock car racing's Super Bowl even though it is the first official race of the year. Daytona and Talladega in Alabama are stock car racing's only true super-speedways. They are long (each at least 2½ miles) with steeply-angled racing surfaces, and they are fast. Drivers sometimes reach speeds of nearly 200 miles per hour with their cars only inches apart.

D is also for drafting. Because the tracks at Daytona and Talladega are so large and speed is so important, drivers must use this technique. Drafting is when drivers race in a single file to share airflow. Cars can go faster if they cut through the air more easily. The first car punches an imaginary hole through the air, and the following cars use it to their advantage.

D d

E is for Dale Earnhardt,
famous number 3,
a champion whose untimely end
came so suddenly.

When Dale Earnhardt was killed after crashing into the wall on the last lap of the 2001 Daytona 500, it was a tragic end to a legendary career. Driving his famous black #3 Chevrolet, Earnhardt was known as "The Intimidator" because of his aggressive style of driving. He shares the record for most NASCAR championships (seven) and won 76 races in his 27-year career. Earnhardt followed his father, Ralph, into the stock car circuit and was later followed by his son, Dale Jr., who has become one of the most popular drivers in the Nextel Cup Series. "Junior" won the 2004 Daytona 500.

The Jarretts—Ned, Dale, and Jason—are another successful three-generation stock car family. In addition, several sets of brothers have made stock car racing a family business, including the Wallaces (Rusty, Mike, and Kenny), the Bodines (Geoffrey, Brett, and Todd), the Labontes (Terry and Bobby), the Waltrips (Darrell and Michael), the Burtons (Jeff and Ward), and the Busch brothers (Kurt and Kyle).

A stock car race can't begin or end without the flagman, who is perched atop a flag stand about 15 or 20 feet above the finish line. Each flag color communicates something specific to the drivers, including green (start the race), yellow (slow down because there is trouble on the track), and red (stop the race because of an emergency or because the track is too wet or damaged to continue). If the flagman waves a black flag when a specific driver passes him, it means the driver either broke the rules or has something wrong with his car, such as an oil leak. He must get off the track and report to pit road. A blue flag with a diagonal stripe signals to a driver that he is a lap behind the leaders and should let them pass. When the lead driver enters his final lap, the flagman waves a white flag. And, of course, a checkered flag announces that the winner has just crossed the finish line.

F f

F is for the Flagman
standing just above the track
and waving flags of green or red,
yellow, white, or black.

G is the guys in the Garage,
who are a special breed.
They get all greasy making sure
the cars are up to speed.

Each car has only one driver, but he has dozens of teammates—from the fellow who sweeps the floors of the garage to the owner who hires the race team. These days, most owners actually own more than one car in a race, and many have become nearly as famous as their drivers. The crew chief, the leader of the team, often works longer hours than anyone. He decides which changes to make to a car during race weekend and which strategies to use during a race. The car chief works closely with the crew chief to make sure this is done. Other team members who work around the garage (in matching team uniforms) include engine specialists, general mechanics, and engineers. Among the behind-the-scenes team members are engine builders, tire specialists, parts specialists, fabricators (who mold the car's metal frame into shape), and even people who drive the team's equipment from racetrack to racetrack.

H h

Safety is a vital part of stock car racing because accidents are common and can be life-threatening. Drivers wear fire-resistant jumpsuits and padded helmets, as well as gloves and insulated shoes to protect their hands and feet from the intense heat of a stock car. The cars contain no glass that might shatter during an accident, so there are no headlights, taillights, or side windows. The front and rear windshields are made of shatterproof plastic. A stock car has only one seat, and the driver's seat is custom-fitted to his body to protect him from being jarred around. Once seated, the driver straps himself in with a five-point seatbelt—five belts that come together at the center of his chest. A mesh window net is fastened over the driver's window opening to keep his head and arms inside the vehicle. His seat is also surrounded by a roll cage made of steel, which protects him from getting crushed if his car flips or tumbles.

Racing is quite dangerous. That's why **H** can be a Harness and a Helmet to ensure safety.

Most fans watch races from the grand-stands, but many racetracks allow fans into the infield—the large grassy area in the middle of the racing oval. Fans often drive their cars, pickup trucks, or motor-homes into the infield. Then they watch the race while sitting on top of them. Often, people camp there for the entire weekend.

I is also for inspection. To make sure that one specific car or car brand doesn't have an advantage on the track, NASCAR creates many regulations. Officials conduct a technical inspection (called tech) of each car several times during a race weekend to be sure that every team is following the rules, whether the rule is about the size of a gas tank (called a fuel cell), the weight of the car (Nextel Cup cars must weigh at least 3,400 pounds), the setup of the engine, or safety considerations. Even after a race, the top five cars must be inspected again.

I

I Stand inside the oval.
is the Infield grass.
You're closer to the action
as you watch the racers pass.

I i

When his car needs gas, fresh tires, or mechanical repairs, a driver makes a pit stop along pit road. Only seven members of the race team are allowed to work on the car during a pit stop. This "over-the-wall crew" includes one jackman (who uses a jack to lift the car), two tire carriers, two tire changers, one gas man (who fills the tank), and one catch can man (who holds a container to collect overflowing gas). A pit stop can win or lose the race for a team. One second may make the difference, so pit crews practice constantly. A good pit stop with four tire changes can take as little as 15 seconds, but teams may also choose a two-tire stop or a gas-and-go (gas only).

J is also for Jeff Gordon, who already had won four series championships, three Daytona 500s, and more than 70 races by the time he was 33 years old.

J is for the Jackman
    and the rest of the pit crew.
Each has a specific job
    and knows just what to do.

Jj

K Richard Petty is "The King,"
in our alphabet.
He won 200 stock car races.
No one has caught him yet.

Richard Petty is known as "The King" because nobody won more races or did more to promote the sport of stock car racing. Wearing his trademark cowboy hat and dark sunglasses, Petty always made time to talk to fans, pose for pictures, and sign autographs. He was usually smiling because he was often winning, including records of seven Daytona 500 victories and seven series championships. Over his 35-year-career, from 1958 to 1992, he won 200 races—nearly twice as many as any NASCAR driver ever (David Pearson is second with 105). And Petty even finished in second place 158 times! After he won his 200th and final race on the Fourth of July in 1984, his winning #43 Pontiac was displayed at the Smithsonian Institution in Washington, D.C.

Four generations of the Petty family raced stock cars. Richard's father, Lee, was victorious in the first Daytona 500 in 1959 and won the series championship three times. Richard's son, Kyle, and grandson, Adam, also became well-known drivers.

In most races, drivers compete by circling the track counterclockwise. That means every turn is a left turn. Each time around the oval is considered a lap. A car that is completing the same lap as the leader is said to be on the lead lap. Some racetracks require long laps (at Talladega Super-speedway, each is 2.66 miles) and others are much shorter. At Bristol Motor Speedway in Tennessee, it takes cars only about 15 or 16 seconds to go around the oval. The track is nicknamed "The World's Fastest Half-Mile."

Another L is lights. Most Nextel Cup events take place on Sunday afternoons. But more and more, racetracks are hosting lighted races on Saturday or Sunday evenings. Drivers often like the events because they don't get as hot inside the cars. Fans love it because they often see sparks shooting into the air like fireworks.

Ll

There's no need for directions
and no use for a map.
L is drivers turning Left
to complete a lap.

M m

Traveling from track to track, always on the roam, drivers take their house with them. **M** is a Motorhome.

Racing events are held at speedways all across the country—from California to New Hampshire. Drivers may be away from home more than 100 days each year. Drivers and their families may travel by airplane to a town, then stay in a luxurious motorhome that has been driven there (and stocked with food) by a member of their race team. These vehicles are parked in a motorhome lot reserved for drivers and crew chiefs.

M is also for miles. Although the name of a stock car event sometimes describes the number of laps to be raced around the track, it usually describes how many miles are to be covered. For instance, the Brickyard 400 is a 400-mile race at famed Indianapolis Motor Speedway. The longest race on the Nextel Cup schedule is the 600-mile Coca-Cola 600 at Lowe's Motor Speedway in Charlotte, North Carolina.

Another **M** is midget cars. Midgets are miniature, lightweight open-wheel cars with no fenders. Quarter midgets are the smallest version, which many kids squeeze into for their first racing experience. Three-quarter midgets are slightly larger. Midgets are the largest and fastest cars in the class. Midget races are generally short (no more than 25 miles) on quarter-mile or half-mile tracks.

The National Association for Stock Car Auto Racing (NASCAR) stages races and makes the rules for nearly a dozen racing series. The Busch Series, which holds most of its races on Saturday, is a competitive series where many of the nation's top drivers gain experience before competing in the Nextel Cup Series (NASCAR's version of the major leagues). Most drivers start their careers on short, dirt tracks near their homes and in regional leagues like the Busch North Series.

N is also for numbers. Each stock car has its own number, and people often use the number instead of the name of the driver when talking about a car. For instance, they'll say, "The 40 is the fastest car out there today."

Another **N** is nicknames. Racing legends include "The Iron Man" (Terry Labonte), "Fireball" (Glenn Roberts), and "Million Dollar Bill" (Bill Elliott). Some famous racetracks are known as "The Brickyard" (Indianapolis Motor Speedway), "The Rock" (North Carolina Speedway), and "The Monster Mile" (Dover International Speedway).

N NASCAR and the Nextel Cup.
can stand for those
and a nifty late-race passing move
to nab victory by a nose.

Most speedways are the shape
of an Oval. That's our O.
Watch the cars speed 'round the turns,
engines roaring as they go.

Most races are held on oval-shaped tracks. The strip of racetrack where the start/finish line is located is called the frontstretch or front straightaway. The backstretch or back straightaway is on the opposite side of the track. These are connected by sweeping turns at both ends. On a traditional oval track, drivers must make four turns to complete a lap. However, there are also tri-ovals with a tiny extra turn, quad-ovals with two extra turns, a triangular track (Pocono Raceway in Pennsylvania), and road courses.

In Nextel Cup racing there are a few short tracks (where there is much bumping and banging), two long superspeedways (where speed is vital), and many intermediate tracks (which combine elements of both). Each racetrack has its own challenges. The racing surface may be smooth or bumpy, wide or narrow, flat or high-banked (meaning the racetrack is steeply sloped). In fact, tiny Bristol Motor Speedway in Tennessee is so high-banked that drivers compare it to piloting a speedboat around a toilet bowl.

Oo

P p

P is for the Pace Car,
which leads the racing pack.
Watch the cars speed up
as it veers off the track.

The pace car is an official vehicle that keeps the stock cars at safe speeds during warm-up laps, accidents, and restarts. Once a pace car enters the track, all other drivers must match its speed. Each NASCAR race begins with a "flying start," which means the cars are in motion when the race officially begins. The pace car leads the field around the track at slower speeds until the flagman waves the green flag to start the race. Then the pace car veers off into pit road and the racing begins. Although celebrities are often allowed to drive the pace car at the beginning of a race, the drivers who do it after an accident are obviously quite experienced.

P is also for David Pearson, who won three NASCAR series championships and 105 races in his remarkable career. Only Richard Petty won more. Because of his cunning racing style, Pearson's nickname was the "Silver Fox."

Forty-three cars are allowed to participate in each Nextel Cup race, but the drivers have to prove their worth by qualifying. They complete one lap around the track (sometimes two), and their time determines their place on the starting grid, which includes 21 rows of two cars and a single car in the back row. The fastest qualifier, called the pole winner (or pole sitter), starts on the inside of the front row. The second-fastest starts on the outside of the front row, and so on. The fastest and slowest cars are often separated by less than one second. Qualifying usually takes place on Friday before a Sunday race. Before and after qualifying, race teams practice and tinker with their cars to improve the speed.

Q q

Q is the Quest to Qualify,
a driver's early mission.
Complete a lap quickly enough
to grab the pole position.

R is Radio contact
between a driver and his crew.
A race isn't just turning left.
There's strategizing, too.

A driver remains in two-way radio contact with his crew chief throughout the race. They discuss how the car is handling, when to make a pit stop, and other strategies. Drivers also keep in contact with teammates called spotters, who sit high above the racetrack to get a full view of the race. When a spotter sees that there is room to pass another car on the outside (the right or high side of the track), he tells the driver to "Clear high!" Or he says "Clear low!" for a pass on the inside. Spotters also alert the drivers about accidents and tell them where to go on the track to avoid it.

Fans at stock car events actually can rent or buy radio scanners that allow them to listen to the conversations between driver and crew during practice, qualifying, and the race itself. It's a bit like standing in the huddle while an NFL quarterback calls the play!

On May 1, 1987, at Talladega Superspeedway in Alabama, driver Bill Elliott set an all-time speed record for stock cars. He won the pole position for the Winston 500 by recording a blazing speed of 212.808 miles per hour. It was so fast that officials feared it was unsafe. They soon changed the rules to reduce speeds at the largest, fastest racetracks.

S is also for sponsors, which are a huge part of stock car racing. It costs millions of dollars to run a racing team each year, so team owners reduce expenses by getting large companies to sponsor their race teams. The companies place their name and logo on the team uniforms and on the stock cars, which become very fast-moving billboards selling everything from motor oil to M&M's. Many races are sponsored by huge companies, too, such as the Pepsi 400 and the Checker Auto Parts 500. Even entire racing leagues rely on sponsorship. The Nextel Cup is sponsored by Nextel Communications.

S s

S must stand for Speed, of course,
    a stock car's stunning power.
Sometimes it seems just a blur
    at 200 miles per hour.

In 1995 the Craftsman Truck Series began, in which drivers race specially-designed pickup trucks that are about two feet longer and 12 inches shorter in height than typical passenger trucks.

South Carolina's Darlington Raceway, built in 1950, has been called "The Track Too Tough to Tame." Turn 4 at the racetrack is so narrow that drivers often scrape the wall, which leaves a strip of paint known as the famous "Darlington Stripe."

T is also for tires, tread, and traction. The tires on stock cars are wider than those on your family car, and they don't have any tread (the grooved part of the tire). This is because stock cars need traction to grip the track, so they need as much tire rubber touching the road as possible.

Another **T** is tachometer. NASCAR stock cars don't have speedometers to show how fast they're going. Instead, drivers check a tachometer, which indicates how hard an engine is working by measuring its revolutions per minute—or RPM.

T is NASCAR Craftsman Trucks
and a track of longtime fame.
Darlington Raceway is a special T.
It's called "Too Tough to Tame."

Look Under the hood.
That's a task for **U**.
Marvel at the engine
and what it can do.

Stock car engines are built to endure long races and to produce a lot of horsepower, a unit of measurement representing how much power an engine generates. Engines in Nextel Cup cars generate about 750 horsepower, while Busch Series engines produce about 550 horsepower. A carburetor is the part of the engine where air and fuel mix. If the flow of air is reduced, the engine generates less horsepower, which means less speed. At stock car racing's two fastest racetracks, Daytona and Talladega, officials have tried to reduce speeds in order to increase safety. So every race team at these superspeedways is required to install a restrictor plate, a thin metal plate with four holes that is placed atop the carburetor to limit the flow of air.

U u

V is for the View
from the driver's seat.
Feel the strong vibrations
and the stifling heat.

Have you ever wondered what it must be like to drive a stock car at more than 150 miles per hour? It's incredibly challenging! While speeding around the track, drivers must shift gears quickly, turn the steering wheel gently, and remain focused for as many as four hours and 600 miles. Drivers must think quickly, too. They have to know when to drive aggressively or patiently, when to pass the car in front of them, whether to pass on the inside or outside, and how to take the fastest route around the racetrack.

In a stock car, there is no air-conditioning, and driving is quite a feat of endurance. Drivers can turn a switch to blow cool air into their helmet and through holes in their seat, but it still gets extremely hot, often above 120 degrees. Because they wear so much safety equipment, drivers have been known to lose as much as ten pounds by sweating during a race.

Two racetracks, Watkins Glen International in New York (known as "The Glen") and Infineon Raceway in California, are special because they are road courses. These can be just about any shape and include several gradual turns and some sharp turns in both directions. The event at Watkins Glen was originally a sports car race through the streets of the village in central New York.

W is also for women. The most famous words in auto racing are: "Gentlemen, start your engines!" However, women also have been successful drivers, including Janet Guthrie, who finished 12th in the 1977 Daytona 500. Women also make up about half of the fans attending stock car races.

Another **W** is Darrell Waltrip, who earned the nickname "Jaws" back in the 1980s because he talked a lot. But as a driver, he also won a lot—84 times in his career. Today he talks all he wants as a popular TV broadcaster.

W is the Watkins Glen road course in New York State. It started with a race through town in 1948.

X is in eXcitement,
   which describes all stock car races
and all the loyal fans
   with wide smiles on their faces.

Attending a race is an experience that shocks all your senses. You can see the cars racing by in a colorful parade, feel the grandstands shake, and smell the odor of burned rubber and gasoline. And even if you're wearing earplugs (which are necessary for protecting your ears), you can still hear the loud roar of the powerful engines as the cars zoom by at tremendous speeds. Driver Mark Martin once described it as sounding like "giant-sized bees flying a million miles an hour."

As many as 400,000 fans may attend a single Nextel Cup race. Unlike most sporting events in which you root for one team or the other, fans cheer for their favorite of the 43 drivers. They may show their support for Jimmie Johnson, for example, by wearing a #48 jacket or jersey. Stock car fans are some of the most loyal fans in the world.

X

X

Y, the Yellow flag, signals
to drivers, crew, and crowd
that it's time to slow down.
No passing is allowed.

The yellow flag is also known as the caution flag. It is waved when drivers need to slow down because there is trouble on the racetrack. Often, this means there was an accident, or perhaps there is oil or other unsafe material on the track. The drivers return to the start/finish line without passing any other cars. Then they follow a pace car around the track until the caution is over. Often, drivers will take the opportunity to make a much-needed pit stop.

Y is also for Cale Yarborough, who is the only driver ever to win three series championships in a row (from 1976 to 1978). He was a four-time Daytona 500 winner, and his 83 victories rank fifth-best all-time. Yarborough also set records by winning five straight events in 1976 and by qualifying for 14 pole positions in 1980.

Z is the Zebra-colored flag
checkered black and white
and waving at the finish line,
quite a welcome sight!

The checkered flag is one of the most famous sights in sports, and stock car finishes can be some of the most dramatic. Rules are closely monitored so that no car has an unfair advantage over the competition, and often this results in extremely close races. Sometimes drivers may race hard for 500 miles and still finish inches apart.

After a driver wins a race, he usually circles the track one more time while waving to the fans. Then he heads to Victory Lane, which isn't really a lane. It is actually a roped-off area located in the infield where the race team, sponsors, and their families celebrate a win. Finally, after a week of traveling, practicing, tinkering with the car, qualifying, tinkering again, strategizing, and then racing for several hours and hundreds of miles, the team gets to enjoy a mission accomplished. Of course, next week they have to do it all over again.

Zz

Brad Herzog

Brad Herzog lives on California's Monterey Peninsula with his wife Amy and his two sons, Luke and Jesse. As a freelance writer, Brad has won several awards from the Council for Advancement and Support of Education, including a Grand Gold Medal for best article of the year. His articles about auto racing have covered subjects as diverse as NASCAR's full-time flagman, the origins of the Watkins Glen road race, and the achievements of paraplegic racers.

Brad began his writing career as a sports reporter at a small newspaper in upstate New York, not far from Watkins Glen. He has since published more than two-dozen books, including two memoirs about his travels through small-town America and four other books for Sleeping Bear Press—*K is for Kick: A Soccer Alphabet*; *H is for Home Run: A Baseball Alphabet*; *T is for Touchdown: A Football Alphabet*; and *P is for Putt: A Golf Alphabet*. He is also the author of *The Sports 100*, which ranks the one hundred most important people in United States sports history (including Bill France and Richard Petty).

Jane Gilltrap Bready

Born in Australia, Jane Gilltrap Bready developed a passion for cars and racing because of the proximity of her grandfather's automobile museum. Jane's artwork has depicted many forms of auto racing, and she has worked with many of motorsports' top teams. Jane has been a NASCAR licensed artist since 1998. She lives in New Hampshire with her husband Mike, and their children, Gemma and Ian. Jane will be donating a portion of her royalties from this project to the Victory Junction Gang Camp in Randleman, North Carolina. The camp enriches the lives of children with chronic medical conditions or serious illnesses. Kyle and Pattie Petty are the founders of Victory Junction.